WE CALL OURSELVES *Disciples*

WE CALL OURSELVES *Disciples*

Edited by
KAMILAH HALL SHARP
& JOEL BROWN

chalice
PRESS

Scriptures are from the *New Revised Standard Version*, Updated Edition, unless otherwise noted.

Print: 9780827243491

EPUB: 9780827243507

EPDF: 9780827243514

ChalicePress.com

Table of Contents

Introduction

When fellow followers of Christ meet and begin to share our faith stories, one of the first words used will often be the name of a denomination, a religious group that has its own shared values and beliefs that are unique or slightly different from other Christian groups. Many Christians instinctively seek to determine what differentiates one denomination from another.

We who call ourselves *Disciples*, however, are more likely to seek what our denominations and our faiths have in common. Being part of the Disciples technically, members or adherents to the Christian Church (Disciples of Christ), also abbreviated as the DOC, the denomination's formal name—has the roots of Christianity in a single church, sharing common values, recognizing the diversity of theology and practice, honoring God's love for all, and holding communion at the center of a shared faith.

In this book, you will find twelve chapters written by Disciples pastors and scholars, on the ways Disciples view and live in each topic. "Ways" is plural because Disciples have diverse views and practices. Throughout the book, the authors address Disciples' diversity, which is not limited to gender, sex, race, sexuality, or socioeconomic status. Although diversity is a staple in the denomination and in these essays, unity is a common goal. The beauty of this is that there can be unity within diversity; we do not have to be the same because God's creation is diverse.

We Call Ourselves Disciples begins with "The Disciples and the Bible," because the Bible is foundational for Disciples. Ron Allen explains the history of interpretation and the diversity in the DOC. He acknowledges that there is agency in interpretation and a need for humility as he calls for readers to reengage the Bible.

"Social Justice as Embodied in Micah 6:8" examines the meaning of justice in the Bible and our call as Disciples to engage in embodied social justice. Noting that the call to be the hands and feet of Jesus is grounded in the biblical text, readers are challenged to move beyond charity toward justice.

In "Doing Theology," José Morales describes the diversity in the approaches of Disciples' theology, how we think and talk about God. He envisions beauty in our diversity because the vastness of God requires more than one way. The diversity of Disciples' theology is not problematic but deepens our theological thinking.

"Liturgy and Worship" author Nathan Russell presents the variety of ways that Disciples worship in their local congregations. Although each church determines its expressions in worship, some commonalities exist in some aspects of worship—namely, music, prayer, preaching, and sacrament. Further, each of these is done in the presence of God and the community for worship.

In "The Baptized Life," Chris Wilson tunes into specific sacraments of the church as he discusses the sacred encounter of the divine and humanity during baptism. He explains the evolution of the Disciples' view of when baptism should occur and the meaning behind the decision to be baptized. There is celebration, affirmation, and connection for the one being baptized and for the community.

In "Communion," Terri Hord Owens explains Disciples' commitment to full access to communion for all. She considers the significance of the elements and communion in general, while proposing the impact a table open to those who lead and partake could make in the world.

In "Christian Unity: Our Polar Star," Disciples ecumenist Paul Tché explores the movement's foundational commitment to the unity of the entire church, which is rooted sacramentally in the Lord's table. Tché documents how this commitment has shaped the church's identity, mission, and structure as Disciples strive to live in a way that demonstrates oneness with God and one another.

In "Diversity and Inclusion," Eli Rolón Jeong discusses how Disciples' commitment to unity, which is rooted in the practice of the Lord's table, has contributed to the church's work for inclusion. Disciples have increasingly committed themselves to intentional inclusion across racial, ethnic, gender, sexual, and cultural identities, emphasizing our diversity amid unity as a gift rather than a challenge.

The tension between diversity and unity is ever-present in Disciples history. In "Turning Points in Disciples History," Joel Brown traces how Disciples time and again reordered themselves to better pursue the sense of mission to which God was calling the church. Brown examines key events and emphasizes that Disciples' faithfulness arises from embracing diversity within their ongoing pursuit of unity.

In "Global Ministries," LaMarco Cable traces the 175-year evolution of Disciples' international mission, from evangelistic outreach to mutual partnership, emphasizing solidarity, justice, and cooperation. Cable highlights the church's collaboration with the United Church of Christ and demonstrates Disciples' current commitment to equitable global engagement, decolonization, leadership development, and authentic partnership in global missions.

In "Congregations and Their Pastors," Katie Hays explores the diverse-yet-common life of Disciples congregations, identifying several of their essential functions—worship, prayer, theological reflection, friendship, harmony, and blessing. Disciples congregations are intentional communities seeking to live out their discipleship of Jesus together. Pastoral leaders are those called to help congregations live into this vision, not as a congregation's boss but as its servant.

The final essay, LaTaunya Bynum's "A Brief Overview of Our Polity," describes the covenant-based polity (i.e., "church structure") of the DOC, stressing the tension between congregational interconnectedness and self-governance. The church exists in congregational, regional, and general expressions. By highlighting covenant as relational rather than contractual, Bynum illustrates how Disciples practice shared authority and accountability in a diverse church committed to unity and wholeness.

We hope Disciples who are new to the tradition, as well as those who have long called this movement home, will encounter the chapters here as neither prescriptive nor descriptive of Disciples doctrines and practices but, rather, as an invitation to enter into an ongoing conversation. This dialogue opens space for considering the diverse ways Disciples have thought about and practiced their faith. Although this diversity can feel messy and challenging at times, it is precisely in our willingness to dwell within these differences and tensions that we move closer to our shared vision of unity. It is in embracing this complexity, faithfully holding together the many and varied threads of our identity, that we live into our calling as Disciples of Christ, co-laborers with God in the pursuit of unity and wholeness in the church and in the world.

Disciples and the Bible

Ronald J. Allen

"Diversity" describes many aspects of Disciples life, including our relationships with the Bible in both past and present. Although all Disciples recognize the Bible as an authority for the church, there is no single Disciples approach to the Bible. Disciples have different perspectives on the nature of the Bible itself, on how to interpret it, and on how the church relates the Bible to other sources of authority.

In the first generation of Disciples (roughly 1804 through the Civil War), many people believed the leading ideas in the Bible contained divine revelation. Many followed Alexander Campbell in seeing the biblical material divided into three periods: (1) the ancestors in Genesis; (2) from Moses to the day of Pentecost; and (3) the Christian era, beginning on the day of Pentecost and continuing into the present. Few Disciples today continue this way of thinking.

To early Disciples, the most authoritative parts of the Bible were the writings that came *after* Pentecost. Campbell saw these materials as a constitution for the church, revealing its identity and instructing its worship, governance, and mission. The biblical writings that document the time before Pentecost—including the gospels—had less authority. By contrast, contemporary Disciples usually regard the whole Bible as having authoritative qualities, with some Disciples prioritizing the gospels.

Alexander Campbell thought the church should interpret the Bible by taking account of historical context, authorship, literary devices, and the intentions of the document. It was particularly important for interpreters to "come within the understanding distance"—that is, readers should interpret the Bible from the standpoint of being existentially aware of God's unrelenting love and God's larger purposes. Interpretation should take place in community to benefit from the insights of the different participants.

For many people, the understanding distance included the notion of postmillennialism, the idea that the mission of the church includes preparing the world for the return of Christ by engaging in social reform designed to reshape the social world in love, peace, and prosperity. Only after this effort would Christ return to rule. The church, then, reads the Bible for guidance in how to prepare the church and the world for the final return of Christ. Although few Disciples today subscribe to postmillennialism, there is a thematic similarity between the focus on social reform in postmillennialism and the concern for justice permeating current Disciples life.

Two important developments occurred following the Civil War and into the early twentieth century. These phenomena continue in modified forms today.

In one development, a stream of scholarship, often called *higher criticism*, taught that the Bible contains human interpretations of the events and ideas within it. Indeed, the Bible is not a singular volume but a library whose books were shaped and reshaped over several centuries and include viewpoints that differ with one another. Moreover, the Bible does not assume a scientific view of the world but offers theological interpretations of the meaning of life in language that is often figurative, poetic, allegorical, analogical, and mythic. A major concern here is to find a faith that is at home in the scientific worldview. As a friend puts it, "I want a faith that makes sense in light of the way I think about the world today."

The other development was a reaction against higher criticism. According to this camp, divine inspiration means that the Bible is factually true in almost every regard (except for figurative language). Conservative evangelicals are today's heirs of this movement. Although evangelicals themselves have diverse views on the degree to which the Bible is inspired, these Disciples believe the church largely needs to understand what the Bible says and then apply that message.

Additional patterns of biblical interpretation are present among Disciples today. One is a liberation approach. These interpreters note that many communities—especially women, people of color, and LGBTQA+ communities—suffer injustice from racism, sexism, heterosexism, economic exploitation, and multiple other oppressions. Liberation interpreters read the Bible to help identify and critique sources of oppression and to empower communities to join God in struggling for liberation.

Many non-Eurocentric congregations approach the Bible from the perspective of their own social locations. Such congregations often note three things.

1. The cultures in the Bible often differ in some ways from their own cultures.
2. At the same time, their cultures sometimes share biblical assumptions in ways that Eurocentric cultures do not. For example, collective identity in the biblical world often resonates with similar qualities in contemporary non-European settings.
3. Until recently, much biblical interpretation in trans-Euro communities assumed Eurocentric assumptions and methods. Instead, these interpreters now begin with their own cultural values, sometimes translating concepts from the Bible into their own categories and sometimes using elements of the Bible to interpret aspects of their cultural experience. These emphases typically include concern for liberation. Such approaches occur among African Americans, Hispanics, Koreans, Haitians, and others. Women often

interpret the Bible in light of their distinctive concerns, for example, womanists (African Americans) and *mujeristas* (Latinas).

The social world today is highly polarized. Public discourse often devolves into name-calling, demonizing, and worse. In this hostile setting, Disciples have the opportunity to deal with interpretive differences in ways that make a witness. According to our tradition, biblical interpretation should occur in the midst of a mutually supportive community. Alexander Campbell identified humility as a key in this process. This approach, infused by respect for the other and by seeking the optimum common good, can be a model for other communities in this fractious world.

For the Bible to continue to have a formative role in Disciples life, it must be a living part of our theological worldviews. Except for sermons, my impression is that many Disciples today have little serious interaction with the Bible. Given the many turgid issues of our moment in history, the time is ripe to engage the Bible afresh.

Social Justice as Embodied in Micah 6:8

Kamilah Hall Sharp

Micah 6:8 is a verse familiar to many people. What does God require of us mere mortals? This is the question the prophet Micah raises to the people of Israel as God brings a case against them. The courtroom drama unfolds with God telling the people all God has done for them and a reply questioning what they should do to please God. The answer is straightforward—do justice, love kindness, and walk humbly with God. What does this mean, particularly in the Christian Church (Disciples of Christ), for those who commit to following Jesus, a brown-skinned Palestinian Jew who was forced to go to a foreign land for his own safety as a child, fed the hungry, and flipped tables in protest of injustice?

To understand how to do justice, one must first understand what justice is. The Hebrew term translated as justice in this verse is *mishpat*, which occurs more than four hundred and twenty times in the Hebrew Bible. It can be translated as justice, judgment, legal right, or a just measure. The numerous mentions of the word throughout the Bible indicate its importance. Clearly, God is concerned about justice, and doing justice pleases God. There is a difference between justice and charity. If there were more justice, there would be less need for charities. When one goes to serve food to those who are unsheltered and/or food insecure, that is charity. Addressing the issues that cause our siblings to be unsheltered and hungry is justice work. Although charity makes us feel good about giving and should be done, we are called to do more; we are called to do justice, especially social justice.

Social justice is grounded in the Bible. It involves righting the relationships for people and all of God's creation with systems and humankind. Community is centered in the biblical text as it provides instructions and illustrations on our relationships with God and with one another. When the focus is shifted to the needs and good of the whole community, instead of the individual, social justice is imperative. It requires giving of ourselves for that beyond us for the love of all. Social justice is not simply charity or social service.

"Do" is a verb, a word of action. For people to *do* justice requires an embodiment of justice in a way that is spiritual, visible, and tangible. Embodied social justice is being moved by the spirit to be the hands and feet of God to make the beloved kin-dom seen and felt as real. Thus, although our voices are essential in doing social justice, our words alone are not sufficient. Embodied social justice requires action beyond resolutions. Our words with actions show the love of a living God in a world that desperately needs it and embodies justice.

How does this happen for Disciples? Given that Disciples are part of the Stone-Campbell movement—which was the largest slaveholding religious body in the United States per capita—like all major denominations, it has a complicated history it must continue to acknowledge and grapple with. Some Disciples churches embrace and live into the call to embody social justice, and others do not. Disciples ministers and laypersons participated in the Underground Railroad, the women's suffrage movement, and the March on Washington for Jobs and Freedom; others worked on the passage of the Civil Rights Acts of 1964 and much more. These Disciples chose to do justice, love kindness, and walk humbly with God, even at the risk of death.

To be clear, the work of embodied social justice is challenging and can come at a cost; thus, it warrants courage. Therefore, Disciples must remember that others accepted the challenge and the call from God "to do" justice, and "doing" embodied social justice is following Jesus. When Jesus walked the Earth, he fed hungry people, healed those who were sick, and challenged the empire. As a result, there were those who followed him and those who wanted him killed. Jesus knew the scriptures and God. Jesus loved God and the people. Love is a catalyst for courage to act, and being cognizant of God, who will walk with us, can sustain us.

The Hebrew term *hesed* is used in this verse and is often translated as kindness or steadfast love, which are helpful ways of thinking about what God is requesting. To love kindness or have steadfast love is to show care and concern for others.

Commonly, when the term is used, it is God's *hesed* that is discussed; in other instances, it is when a person or group of persons must extend it to others. God is asking us to love caring for something besides ourselves and offers to walk alongside those who do.

The United States is in a perilous moment, with a strong divide in the population on the best way forward. As changes in laws and policies disrupt and even devastate many people's lives, it behooves us to ask ourselves how Disciples will respond. Will we do more than charity and answer God's call to embody social justice? Moving from charity to justice may feel daunting for some, but it is within reach. Many issues plague our society, and Disciples need to be the hands and feet of God to meet the needs and eliminate the causes. As we continue working to embody social justice, we must ask ourselves: First, does this action show the love of God? And, second, is this a temporary fix, or are we working toward a long-term solution?

When our work shows the love of God for a long-term solution, we follow Jesus and embody social justice. As Disciples, following Jesus is what we are committed to doing, and our actions must align with our commitment so we can have a world in which all of God's children are shown love and can thrive no matter their race, gender, sexuality, economic status, or religion.

Doing Theology

José Francisco Morales Torres

To speak about "how Disciples do theology" is a scary, if not impossible, task. There are many theological approaches within the Disciples' fold. We have liberals, progressives, conservatives, and traditionalists. We have theologians, lay and ordained, who do theology informed by the lived experiences of their respective communities or realities—womanist, Korean-American, and LGBTQIA+ theologians, to name just a few. Disciples theologians work within various theological "schools," such as the Reformed tradition, process thought, neo-orthodoxy, charismatic theology, and many others. Is it therefore impossible to propose a Disciples method for doing theology?

Years ago, I was conversing with Rev. Robert Welsh, president emeritus of what was then the Council of Christian Unity (now Christian Unity and Interfaith Ministry). I asked him the question this chapter seeks to answer: "When gathered with other denominations, how do you represent Disciples *theologically* given that we're so diverse *theologically*?"

First, he embraced this radical welcome to theological diversity as an *essential* part of our way of doing theology. So, this is where I begin: *To do theology in a Disciples way is to begin with, and to remain open to, diverse ways to think about God.* Disciples see theological diversity not as a problem to solve but as a mystery that deepens our theological thinking.

Rev. Welsh added that, as an ecumenical officer, he spoke *from within* our tradition, which is not the same as speaking *for* our tradition. He often used this clause to capture the difference: "It has been the witness of the Disciples of Christ to . . ." This clause acknowledges our theological diversity while affirming predominant features of our life together. For example, *it has been the Disciples' witness to* celebrate holy communion every Sunday. This highlights the common practice at most Disciples congregations of observing holy communion weekly while making room for those congregations that choose a different pattern. For instance, some Haitian congregations celebrate communion once per month after a day of fasting, and some congregations in Puerto Rico celebrate communion weekly but during the midweek service and not on Sunday. Following my colleague's wisdom, I dare to speak *from within* our tradition. In my remaining reflections, I use, explicitly or implicitly, the qualifying phrase to propose, "in fear and trembling," a way of doing theology that cuts across the diversity of Disciples theological expressions.

While embracing theological diversity, it has been the witness of Disciples to do theology grounded in God's word. What do we mean by "God's word"? Well, humans use words to communicate, so "God's word" simply means God speaking to us. But "God-talk" (literal translation of "theo-logy") is never simple and cannot be reduced to human language. This is more than an issue of translation. It is more like God speaks in a kaleidoscope of hundreds of colors, and we are trying to "translate" God's words with a box of eight crayons. Hence, our discernment of what God is saying to us can never be completely certain. This is why being open to theological diversity is crucial. We need all the eight-crayon boxes we can get. Theology is the practice of listening for God's word and interpreting it in a manner that can guide our lives today. And as Christians, we hear God's word most clearly in Jesus Christ, not only in the stories of him in the Bible but also his transforming presence today.

So, when I say "God's word" or "Christ's transforming presence," I bring together three sources of theology: the Bible, worship, and lived experience. Disciples engage the Holy Scriptures with critical rigor yet faithful expectation, seeking their "light" (Psalm 36:9) to understand what God's kaleidoscopic word is for us today. The Bible (word) is a light that guides us to God's word and Christ's living presence (Word).

Generally, taking the Bible seriously has not meant taking it literally, although some Disciples do. Many early Disciples considered it "malpractice" to interpret the Bible without engaging the best biblical scholarship available at the time.

For Disciples, knowing the Bible is not the ultimate goal. The aim of reading scripture is to encounter the living God of Sarah and Mary, speaking to us today through the witness of God's people in the Hebrew Bible and New Testament.

Moreover, it has been the Disciples' witness to necessarily read the scriptures *in community.* God's word for us is discerned most clearly in community. Worship for Disciples is where we read the Bible (the word of God written) *in community*, we hear preaching (the word of God proclaimed) *as community*, and we partake *communally* of the holy communion (the Word of God shared in the bread and cup). All of these spiritual disciplines are communal avenues for encountering the risen Christ—much like the disciples on the road to Emmaus, whose hearts "burned" as Christ explained the scriptures to them and whose eyes recognized Christ in the breaking of the bread. (Luke 24:13–35)

With our theological "hearts" and "eyes" opened through the liturgy framed around the reading of scripture, preaching, and communion, we are oriented and empowered to live the "table way" of life. We are oriented to see Christ in the sharing of the bread of justice and compassion in the world. When we partake of the bread and wine, we not only remember Christ's body broken by the Roman Empire. We consequently heed Christ's imperative to be in solidarity with all bodies broken by the voracious empires running amok in our world. A life dedicated to Christ and to "the least of these" (Matthew 25:40) is a lively way to think about God (i.e., to do theology), because in these acts of solidarity and justice, we encounter God's transforming presence in Christ.

Thus, a Word-mediated—some say, "Christocentric"—approach defines Disciples' way of doing theology. I am not saying we all agree on who Christ is for us. For example, we do not agree on how to theologically explain the relationship between God, Christ, and the Holy Spirit. Disciples theology *requires* a Christology (theology about Jesus Christ) but does not *prescribe* a Christology.

For Disciples, a faithful approach to do theology is deeply attuned to what I call "the ethics of believing." Our witness attests to an ethic of care, to a pastoral concern that we believe combines conviction and humility, confidence and modesty. We resist doctrinal tests of faith for fellowship, except for Peter's confession: "You are the Christ, the Son of the living God" (Matthew 16:16). We do not use creeds to exclude, even if we construct *provisional* affirmations to instruct and inspire. Because we are committed to Church unity, we respect the historic creeds of the Church; we just do not use them as a litmus test for who is in and who is out. Our way of doing theology witnesses to the truth that belief in God means throwing oneself into a Mystery Who cannot be reduced by our eight crayons.

Consequently, *a Disciples way of doing theology affirms that the way we hold a belief also conditions and transforms it.* As Rabbi Yochanan Muffs noted, preserving one's life of faith is like holding a bird in one's hands "tightly enough that it doesn't fly away, gently enough that it isn't choked to death."[1] This rabbinical wisdom is implicit in the Emmaus road story. Yes, we can have confidence in our faith in God because Christ truly appears to us at the table. Yet we must also have modesty because immediately after Christ appears, he *disappears* (Luke 24:31). He disappears *quickly*, before we become arrogant or rigid in our belief and try to color in Christ with our measly eight crayons. Confidently, we follow this way of doing theology with rigor but with openness. Humbly, we do so without predetermined doctrinal outcomes, instead trusting in the Holy Spirit "who blows where She wills" (John 3:8) and letting the theological chips fall where they may.

---

[1] Yochanan Muffs, *The Personhood of God* (Woodstock, VT: Jewish Lights Publishing, 2005), 187.

Liturgy and Worship

Nathan Russell

From the denomination's roots in the Stone-Campbell movement to the present day, the Christian Church (Disciples of Christ) has embodied diverse expressions of how to engage in the liturgy and worship, both of which are the work of the congregation. Early leaders in the movement sought to restore the church to its New Testament roots, suggesting that scripture provided the blueprint for worship. Now, as we move through the twenty-first century, worship in Disciples congregations remains diverse and unscripted, yet people can expect music, prayer, the Word proclaimed, and sacrament—elements that require the active participation of the whole people of God.

Worship is a countercultural act in a world governed by autonomy, capitalism, sin, and death. The cost of dedicating sixty to ninety minutes on a Sunday morning to communal worship is significant, especially in an era in which the individualistic mindset of being "spiritual but not religious" continues to rise. Worship is never a self-centered endeavor; it is the shared work and witness of the gathered church community. Although many denominational forebears have attempted to describe the differing movements of worship, worship cannot be reduced to the mechanics of singing, praying, listening, and communing. Worship transcends the sum of its parts; it leads us toward a yet-to-be-realized promise.

Worship is risky. In *Teaching a Stone to Talk*, Annie Dillard wrote, "we should all be wearing crash helmets. Ushers should issue life preservers and signal flares; they should lash us to our pews. For the sleeping god may wake someday and take offense, or the waking god may draw us out to where we can never return."[1]

Worship provokes the One whom the world has rendered dead to act; worship stirs within the church a passion for the possible. We sing, pray, listen, and commune—risk-filled acts we cannot accomplish on our own—to find the resolve needed to practice resurrection.

Congregational singing has long been an integral part of the Christian Church (Disciples of Christ), although music has not been without controversy. The incorporation of instruments was divisive and contributed to a split within the Stone-Campbell movement. Today, congregational singing in Disciples congregations is accompanied by pipe organ, piano, guitar, percussion, and even prerecorded tracks. The development of printed worship materials like bulletins

---

[1] Annie Dillard, *Teaching a Stone to Talk: Expeditions and Encounters* (New York: HarperCollins, 1982), 48.

and hymnals provided a framework for worship, while the ubiquity of technology and projection screens has expanded the possibilities for new songs.

Singing requires participation. As Stacy Horn wrote in *Imperfect Harmony*, "As long as I'm singing … it's as if I'm inhabiting another reality. I become temporarily suspended in a world where everything bad is bearable, and everything good feels possible."[2]

Although debates over worship style continue, the hope in singing is for the congregation to find its voice through lament and praise.

Liturgy without prayer is incomplete. Throughout a service of worship, numerous prayers are offered: an invocation, intercessory prayers, thanksgiving for the offering, prayer for inspiration, prayer at the communion table, and the recitation of Matthew's version of the prayer that Jesus taught his disciples. Our denominational ancestors held varied understandings of prayer. For instance, Alexander Campbell believed that God does not hear the prayers of those without faith, whereas Barton Stone encouraged people to "pray to be filled with the Holy Spirit of God as a way to be quickened in the ways of God."[3] Prayer in worship rides on the shared

[2] Stacy Horn, *Imperfect Harmony: Finding Happiness in the Music of the World* (New York: St. Martin's, 2011), 2.

[3] William O. Paulsell, "Prayer," in *The Encyclopedia of the Stone-Campbell Movement*, eds. Douglas A. Foster, Paul M. Blowers, Jeffrey W. Riddle, and D. Newell Williams (Grand Rapids, MI: Eerdmans, 2004), 601.

breath of the congregation, opening participants to what the Spirit may yet reveal.

Some might suggest that the proclamation of the Word is the main event of worship, but preaching is penultimate. Still, the work of the preacher as a herald of God's good news is essential to the life of the congregation. Although Stone and Campbell rejected some systematized practices of liturgy, many Disciples churches follow the liturgical calendar and use the Revised Common Lectionary, the Narrative Lectionary, or the Women's Lectionary for the Whole Church. Preaching in the Disciples tradition takes many forms. Some ministers focus on the didactic, teaching theological tenants, whereas others are commissioned to return to the congregation with a prophetic message, saying, "Thus saith the Holy One!" Lance Pape aptly described the task of preaching in his book, *The Scandal of Having Something to Say*, by stating,

> Although Christian preaching is grounded in the conviction that a divine commission has authorized a most urgent, winsome, and demanding kind of talk, such talk is not only not warranted to the satisfaction of all those implicated in its claims, but unwarrantable according to any generally accepted public standard. Preaching is, therefore, scandalous talk. It boldly gives offense.[4]

[4] Lance Pape, *The Scandal of Having Something to Say* (Waco, TX: Baylor University Press, 2013), 4.

The stewardship of the pulpit requires that no one enter the congregation with the intent to offend; instead, the preacher speaks with consequence—comforting those who thirst for justice and indicting those who oppress the vulnerable.

Singing, praying, and preaching all lead to the sacrament of communion. Although some Disciples congregations may place the sermon as the final move, communion remains the pinnacle of Christian worship. Communion is a reenactment of Jesus' final meal with his disciples, even as it is a foretaste of the feast that invites all of creation to the table. Disciples congregations practice communion in various ways, including intinction (dipping the bread into the chalice) or the passing of plates with hermetically sealed communion sets. Yet, what is often missing in this sacrament is the acknowledgment of its danger. Weekly participation in the sacrament can easily become routine and innocuous. However, the elements of grain and grape represent the body and blood of Jesus; communion is serious. This eucharistic feast is as costly as it is full of promise—this is communion's danger and joy.

Liturgy and worship are critical aspects of the church's work and witness. Liturgy is the work of the people, even as the liturgy is for all people. Through liturgy and worship inspired by God's inimitable Spirit, the church is drawn closer to the future that God desires and will one day bring to fruition—ultimately leading the whole church to the unbounded promise of a more profound "Alleluia!"

The Baptized Life

Christopher Wilson

> *Sleeper, awake! Rise from the dead, and Christ will shine on you. (Ephesians 5:14)*

Encounters with water shaped and continue to shape the followers of Jesus. Paul's words in Ephesians affirm that baptism awakens the soul to connect us to the world with a deeper passion and desire to reflect the values and life of Jesus. From their origins in the early 1800s, Disciples embraced baptism as a core element of the church and the Christian journey. Baptism is one of the sacred encounters we celebrate with God and a meeting ground between humanity and divinity. Marcus Borg would have named baptism a "thin place" to meet the holy.[1]

The potential power of the baptismal moment for the one being baptized and the whole church is the mystery of that experience connected to water. Water is a symbol of letting

[1] Marcus Borg, *The Heart of Christianity: Rediscovering a Life of Faith* (San Francisco: HarperCollins, 2003), 158.

go, of transition and newness. Memory and significance of a meaningful event is heightened when associated with something tangible like water. People often recall the baptismal font or a natural body of water in which they were baptized. The reflection of baptism joined with the encounter of water strengthens its impact on the believer. We do not assume a magical transformation in that moment, but we claim as people of faith that the moment can inspire our lives in a way that reflects the life and influence of Jesus. We become partners with Jesus and those already baptized to embody and advocate for the kingdom of God and the beloved community. Jesus came to proclaim and invite others to join us.

The founders of our Disciples movement shifted from their former understanding of baptism near birth to baptism happening at an age of understanding. The theological intention invites knowledge of the baptismal experience and how that decision will influence a person's life going forward. We also practice baptism by full immersion, allowing the waters of baptism to cover the whole body of the baptized. Even though this is our practice, we celebrate other forms of baptism when people come to our churches. We recognize baptism as an act of the universal church and not just to a denomination or congregation. We believe God to have a substantial presence in any act of baptism. It is not solely our decision to be baptized. We know God is powerfully present and active in that moment of encounter.

As Disciples have become more involved in the ecumenical movement, baptism has increasingly been understood at its core as an act of the universal church. Baptism is more than individual choice. It is an experience of the individual, God, and the wider church all sharing in this holy act of transformation. It is a fusion of belief covered and strengthened by God's grace. We call it a sacramental moment because it steps into the space of God's mystery and wonder. Baptism includes all the components of a sacramental moment: It conveys grace, strengthens faith, enhances unity and commitment to and with the church, and reassures us of God's promise toward us.

The baptized life is about more than the moment of baptism. Baptism is less a rite of passage to something else and more an entrance into a life of discipleship shaped by the waters of our baptism. Mark Toulouse said of baptism, "Baptism becomes a liturgical opportunity to celebrate a person being baptized, a chance to reaffirm one's baptism, and to teach others the values of what baptism can mean for them in the future."[2]

Claiming our baptismal identity going forward is difficult when the church does not frequently give openings in preaching and liturgical life to help people live into their baptismal vows. We are reminded of this thinking when we recite the words from our Disciples affirmation, which is part of the Preamble to the Design, which declares, "Through

[2] Mark Toulouse, *Joined in Discipleship: The Maturing of an American Religious Movement* (St. Louis, Chalice Press, 1992), 148.

baptism into Christ we enter into newness of life and are made one with the whole people of God."[3]

Baptism is a covenantal encounter. It is about a relationship forged between ourselves, God, and the church. Jesus offers the invitation of baptism to help us see our covenantal identity as one that is stronger than individualism. Baptism, understood as a sacramental moment, is inherently covenantal by nature. Our identity is wrapped up in the identity of others. We are stronger together than we ever are alone. That is why baptisms are encouraged to be larger liturgical moments in the corporate worship experience. Baptisms offer the potential for celebration, affirmation, and a deeper connection to one another and God.

People often look back at their baptism as something they have done and accomplished in their faith journey. Baptism is simultaneously a moment in time and a way of life. Jürgen Moltmann, a German theologian who encourages believers baptism over infant baptism, has advocated that baptism is to be considered a vocational calling for each follower of Jesus.[4] When we look to Jesus as a model for our own baptism, that moment for Jesus propelled him into his ministry. It began his work of proclaiming the good news of God and embodying God's love in the world. Jesus was not baptized to be saved.

---

[3] "The Design of the Christian Church (Disciples of Christ)," Disciples.org, accessed May 21, 2025, https://disciples.org/our-identity/the-design/.

[4] Jürgen Moltmann, *The Church in the Power of the Spirit* (Minneapolis: Fortress Press, 1993), 241-242.

He was baptized to initiate his ministry. Baptism should also "call" us into a life of discipleship and service. For those reared in the church, baptism is an opportunity to deepen our journey of faith.

As we come out of the waters of baptism, we are completely wet. As we leave the baptismal waters, we leave behind wet footprints. Living out our baptismal moment means continuing to walk through life with wet footprints. We desire for our baptism to be a calling upon our lives to strengthen our faith journey. Baptism should awaken us to a new way of engaging the world. We can not only read the words from Ephesians 5:14, we can *embody* them in all that we say and do as a follower of Jesus, "*Sleeper awake! Rise from the dead, and Christ will shine on you.*"

Communion

Terri Hord Owens

The Christian Church (Disciples of Christ) has its historic foundation in the covenant, unity, and inclusion that we celebrate at the Lord's table. Early members of the Presbyterian tradition on the American "frontier" were required to meet with a priest prior to receiving the communion elements. The priest would then give each person a token, indicating that person was "approved" to take communion. The idea that another human being would be in a position to determine one's worthiness to receive the bread and cup was baffling to many, including the future founders of the Disciples, Alexander Campbell and Barton Stone. Such a review was considered a "test of fellowship" that would determine whether one could not only receive communion but also be a member in good standing in the church.

Our commitment to the full inclusion of all God's creation remains an important part of our tradition today. We reject any practice or policy that might be considered a "test of fellowship." Jesus initiated the covenant at the Lord's table and asked us to remember his body and blood each time we partake of these elements.

Christians around the world celebrate the Lord's supper in remembrance of the new covenant that Jesus established on the night he was betrayed.

Luke recounts it with these words:

> When the hour came, he took his place at the table, and the apostles with him. He said to them, "I have eagerly desired to eat this Passover with you before I suffer, for I tell you, I will not eat it until it is fulfilled in the kingdom of God." Then he took a cup, and after giving thanks he said, "Take this and divide it among yourselves, for I tell you that from now on I will not drink of the fruit of the vine until the kingdom of God comes." Then he took a loaf of bread, and when he had given thanks, he broke it and gave it to them, saying, "This is my body, which is given for you. Do this in remembrance of me." And he did the same with the cup after supper, saying, "This cup that is poured out for you is the new covenant in my blood." (Luke 22:14–20, NRSVue; see also Matthew 26:26–30, Mark 14:22–25, and 1 Corinthians 11:23–26)

Jesus took the Jewish meal of Passover and repurposed the elements to create a memory not only for those who followed him during his lifetime on Earth but also those of us who would come to believe in Jesus in future generations. The disciples were familiar with the meal, but now Jesus told them that the bread represented *his* body, and the cup represented *his* blood. While he had spoken of his imminent death, the disciples still did not fully understand what Jesus was saying in that moment. He blessed the bread, and broke it, signifying that his own body would be beaten and broken. When he offered the cup, he invited them to drink, saying that the wine represented his "blood of the covenant, which is poured out for many for the forgiveness of sins."

Christians have many perspectives on the idea of what the blood of Jesus really means, whether Jesus' sacrifice is one of atonement for sin. In Disciples tradition, we believe that, with the help of the Holy Spirit, each one of us can seek understanding and discernment in the scriptures. It is instructive, however, to bear in mind the words of Jesus that are recorded in scripture, as noted in Matthew, Mark, Luke, and 1 Corinthians. We refer to these words of Jesus as "the words of institution." Those who officiate at the table will always use some form of these words as a reminder of what Jesus said when he established this important practice and sacrament.

For Disciples, Jesus is present at the Lord's table as a spiritual presence, serving as our host. We stand to officiate and serve because we have been asked to invite others to share the meal of this new covenant between God and God's creation. Because we do not believe that this sacred meal should be used to distinguish between any of God's beloved, we say in our *Identity Statement:* "[W]e welcome all to the Lord's Table as God has welcomed us." [1]

We also believe that any of us may serve and officiate. You need not be an ordained or commissioned clergy, or even an elder or deacon, to officiate and serve the Lord's supper. In many traditions, only credentialed clergy may serve, and only recognized members of the tradition may partake. Although we believe communion is a believer's meal, we welcome *all* to partake, no matter your tradition or identity. We ask no questions; we invite you to the table.

Most Disciples' congregations observe the Lord's supper each Sunday, and any time we gather, the question is always asked, "Will we have communion?" We are associated with this weekly observance, but it is not the frequency that distinguishes us; it is the commitment to the full access for all to the table of the Lord. It is important also to commit to full access not just to the meal but to the community of God, the covenant that Jesus established when he spoke during that Last Supper.

What an amazing testimony it would be around the world if all Christians were committed to this full access, both to serve and partake. Sadly, differences across Christian traditions regarding who may serve or partake prohibit such

---

[1] "Disciples: Who We Are," Disciples.org, accessed May 19, 2025, https://disciples.org/our-identity/.

a celebration in most situations. As Disciples of Christ, our commitment to unity and inclusion is grounded in our practice at the table. Whenever you eat of the bread and drink of the cup, remember that this covenant between God and God's creation includes all.

Christian Unity: Our Polar Star

Paul S. Tché

> I ask not only on behalf of these but also on behalf of those who will believe in me through their word.
> —John 17:20 (NRSVue)

The Disciples began as a Christian unity movement in the nineteenth century. Troubled by the deep divisions in American Christianity, leaders like Barton Stone and Thomas Campbell—two founders of the Disciples of Christ—sought the unity and oneness of God's church. In his *Declaration and Address*, Thomas Campbell boldly proclaimed, "the Church of Christ upon earth is essentially, intentionally, and constitutionally one."[1] Barton Stone believed that he and his followers were peacemakers, working to heal the divided church as they followed the "polar star" of unity toward the common ground of Christ.

[1] Thomas, Campbell, "Declaration and Address of the Christian Association of Washington" (1809). *Digital Commons, Disciples of Christ Historical Society.* Accessed May 21, 2025, https://digitalcommons.discipleshistory.org/all_foundationaldocuments/7.

This unity movement, born on the frontiers of western Pennsylvania and Kentucky, eventually became a global witness. Its vision of unity, particularly as expressed at the Lord's table, inspired Christians around the world to join the movement. Over the course of the movement, some churches within the Disciples heritage—those inspired first by the *Last Will and Testament of the Springfield Presbytery*, which declared a desire "to die, be dissolved, and sink into union with the Body of Christ at large,"[2] and later by the modern ecumenical movement—went on to join, and even lead, efforts to form uniting and united churches.

At the same time, some churches within our global communion have intentionally chosen not to join other communions in order to maintain a distinctive identity as Disciples. Still, it is clear that, for decades, Disciples churches around the world have remained deeply committed to the pursuit of Christian unity. Although organic union is no longer the goal for many, a shared commitment to visible unity through common mission and ministry remains strong. In these efforts, Disciples have realized that unity is more relational than institutional, and that unity can find its life and reality as Christians worship together and serve

---

[2] Barton Warren Stone and Richard McNemar, "Last Will and Testament of the Springfield Presbytery" (1804). *Digital Commons, Disciples of Christ Historical Society*. Accessed May 21, 2025, https://digitalcommons.discipleshistory.org/all_foundationaldocuments/8.

together.[3] Disciples churches have strived to live in a way that demonstrates oneness with God and one another—so that even those who do not know Christ can see it.

For Disciples, the oneness of Christ's church is essential to God's mission in the world. Without unity, the gospel of reconciliation and healing loses its credibility and witness. A divided church, therefore, becomes a scandal to the world—a contradiction of the very message it proclaims.

Despite our longstanding commitment to Christian unity, perhaps the most painful moments for Disciples come when we are excluded from participation at the eucharistic table. This exclusion grieves us deeply for, from the very beginning, we have understood that unity begins at the Lord's table, where we are already made one in Christ—as Jesus prayed before his crucifixion in the gospel of John. Because unity is a gift given at the table through Christ's sacrifice, and because it is Christ who extends the invitation to his table, Disciples have held firmly that there should be no test of fellowship required to come to the table.

At the beginning of the movement, Alexander Campbell was especially critical of the use of creeds as tests of fellowship, particularly when they were used to bar Christians from the Lord's table. He frequently voiced frustration over how creeds, rather than scripture, had become the basis for determining

---

[3] Robert Welsh, *Basic Understandings of the Disciples of Christ About the Unity We Seek* (Indianapolis: Council on Christian Unity, 2016).

who was welcome in the church. Over time, however, Campbell's stance toward traditional creeds—especially the well-known Apostles' Creed—became more nuanced. By the mid-nineteenth century, he acknowledged the Apostles' Creed as a faithful summary of core Christian beliefs, describing it as more valuable than the many dogmatic formulations produced over the preceding centuries.[4] Today, Disciples identify as a noncreedal tradition not because we deny the truthfulness of these creeds but because we resist the ways they have been used to exclude and divide, especially when they become barriers to full participation in the eucharistic fellowship of Christ.

For this reason, churches in the Disciples tradition have tended to express their faith more in biblical terms. Historically, members would confess their faith by reciting Matthew 16:16. In recent times, many Disciples churches have developed contemporary confessions or affirmations of faith. Because we interpret and reinterpret our faith in light of our own contexts, Disciples can be understood as a "confessing church" rather than simply noncreedal—unbound by fixed affirmations of faith as we seek to respond to God's call in our own time and place.

In the history of Christianity, Christian communions have mostly been defined by their confessions and doctrines. What,

[4] Alexander Campbell, "Reply to Barnabas," *The Millennial Harbinger*, vol. 3, no. 12 (December 1832): 602–604; cf. Robert Cornwall, "Disciples of Christ: Confessing Faith as a Non-Creedal Community," *Discipliana*, vol. 74, no. 1 (2021).

then, makes noncreedal Disciples a distinctive body among Christian communions?

In other words, what binds us together as a distinctive community of faith? It is our sacramental vision of Christian unity. This doesn't simply mean that many Disciples pursue visible unity in any way we can. It means Disciples are particularly called to pursue full eucharistic participation with all Christians. Disciples are called to manifest God-given unity at the Lord's table, where the love of God nourishes all Christians in Jesus Christ, and through that love are made one with one another and with the one, holy, catholic (universal), and apostolic church. So we welcome all who confess Jesus as the Christ, the Son of the living God, and who seek to follow him, at the table—without exception and without hindrance—as God has welcomed us. At the table, we experience communion with God, with Christ, and one another. And that communion becomes our witness to the reconciliation and hospitality we have received.

What defines Disciples is not a particular confession, tradition, doctrine, or practice, but a vision—our sacramental vision of Christian unity that sets us apart as a distinctive community of faith among many Christian denominations. It is the vision we believe was entrusted to us by God as a collective body, one that we continue to hold with deep conviction. It is this vision of unity—in which all followers of Christ will one day gather at the table to share the holy meal—that nourishes and sends us into the world bearing the good news that God loves the world.

It is this vision of unity that grounds us in a shared passion for justice as we remember Christ's work for justice in this world. This vision of unity allows us to embrace diversity not as a threat to unity, but as an expression of it. It is this vision that challenges us to imagine a church broader, deeper, and more ancient than ourselves. And it is this vision of unity that empowers us to claim a larger identity in Christ—one that transcends our boundaries and invites us to live into God's reconciling mission with hope. It is the vision of unity with which Christians encounter other people of faith in order to build a community together and share gifts with one another.

Diversity and Inclusion

Eli Rolón Jeong

For the Christian Church (Disciples of Christ), diversity and inclusion are essential expressions of faith and identity. Like their predecessors, today's Disciples face complex and often contentious racial, ethnic, gender, sexual, religious, and cultural diversity. Although diversity is often considered a challenge, Disciples regard it as an opportunity to live into our vision for welcome and inclusion.

The precept of "wholeness in a fragmented world" helps define Disciples' theology and identity. Our call for unity, particularly at the Lord's table, seeks to integrate diverse elements while affirming each one's uniqueness. A movement for wholeness, in other words, is an active and intentional practice, not merely an end goal.

This vision has shaped Disciples' commitments from the beginning. Barton Stone and Thomas Campbell were committed to Christian unity, breaking down barriers to participation in the Lord's supper. Amid oppression and enslavement, Black Disciples have been establishing congregations affirming the inclusion of African Americans since the beginning of the movement. By the end of the nineteenth century, the movement had women preachers and at least one woman ordained into ministry. Meanwhile, Disciples expanded mission work in Mexico and Texas, and expanded within Chinese and Japanese immigrant communities. Despite widespread discrimination and exclusion, these efforts demonstrate an early commitment to inclusion.

Today, Disciples advance inclusion through their anti-racism/pro-reconciliation initiative, recognizing racism as a spiritual and theological issue requiring systemic change. This initiative challenges Disciples to address and dismantle the structures that produce and uphold injustice, including those within the church, and to move toward racial reconciliation. The National Convocation supports African American leaders and congregations by building on the groundwork of early Black Disciples. Likewise, Obra Hispana responds to the needs of Spanish-speaking communities, and North American Pacific/Asian Disciples (NAPAD) affirms the heritage and gifts of Pacific and Asian peoples. With more than seventeen languages spoken in congregations throughout the United States and Canada, Disciples embody a diverse faith community.

Disciples also work toward LGBTQ+ inclusion. Alliance Q aims to bridge the gap between racial, ethnic, gender, and sexual diversity. Although early efforts were met with resistance, key milestones—such as the affirmation of civil rights for gay and lesbian people in 1977 and the ordination of openly LGBTQ+ ministers in the 1980s and 1990s—reflect ongoing progress. In recent years, resolutions like GA-1327 ("Becoming a People of Grace and Welcome to All") and GA-1929 ("An Invitation to Education for Welcoming and Receiving the Gifts of Transgender and Gender-Diverse People") have demonstrated growing support. Affirmation of the gifts of LGBTQ+ people as participants, leaders, and ordained ministers across the church also continues to grow.

The gospel's profound call for unity drives Disciples' commitment to inclusion. In John 17:20–21, Jesus prays for all believers to be united as one, while Matthew 28:19 mandates a ministry extending to all. Paul warns of the perils of division within the church in 1 Corinthians 10:10 and, conversely, highlights the oneness of the body of Christ in 1 Corinthians 12:13. Thus, unity is not merely a lofty ideal but a practice of mutual respect and support reflecting God's divine image.

For Disciples, the Lord's table is where we practice the call for unity and inclusion. Disciples observe holy communion during weekly services and almost any other time we gather for worship or fellowship. The sacrament is not mandated but offered and celebrated in covenant with anyone professing their faith in Jesus Christ. Although ministers often preside at the table, Disciples empower elders, lay leaders, and youth leaders to lead communion services, further living into a commitment to intentional inclusion. As Disciples "welcome all to the Lord's table as God has welcomed us," the church manifests Christ's united body as it gathers to share a meal in the spirit of openness and against separation.

The Disciples' commitment to diversity and inclusion is not without its challenges. The contentious nature of diversity within the larger societal context is also often reflected in the church's life. Structures of systemic inequality, biases, and injustice are long-standing and complex to dismantle, even for the most faithful and committed individuals and communities. Furthermore, the congregational nature of Disciples polity means that it is up to individuals and congregations to maintain and best exemplify commitments to inclusion in light of diversity. Although Disciples have gained traction in their efforts toward racial reconciliation, affirmation of women and LGBTQ+ folks, and inclusion in general, many Disciples may still hold varied levels of understanding, commitment, or willingness to be fully inclusive of historically marginalized groups of people.

Yet, Disciples demonstrate that inclusion is possible. Engaging diversity requires humility, curiosity, and wisdom. Recognizing when diversity enriches rather than divides us strengthens the church's mission. Courage is necessary to identify and confront exclusion driven by fear, hate, and harm. Disciples uphold justice with confidence, striving to build communities in which diverse voices are present, heard, and valued—ensuring that the diversity present in our context fully participates in the life of the church.

Inclusion calls for creativity and resourcefulness. It is about forming meaningful and harmonious relationships and fostering new possibilities for flourishing and thriving. By valuing diversity, Disciples create opportunities for collaboration, integrating diverse fragments without losing their unique meaning and significance.

Embracing diversity and building a faithful, unified community is a significant priority that demands time, intention, and care. It demands recognizing and reaffirming shared core values while maintaining and respecting distinct identities. Diversity and inclusion within the Christian Church (Disciples of Christ) do not blur fragments but embrace them as unique elements essential to building wholeness.

Turning Points in Disciples History

Joel Brown

It is perhaps a fool's errand to attempt to tell a singular history of Disciples, whether in a few pages or a few hundred. Historians must constantly decide what to include and what to leave out. When this is uncritically undertaken, it results in historical narratives that reflect the concerns and identities of those who study them—often White and male—while marginalizing or erasing the contributions of non-White, non-male Disciples. As Sandhya Rani Jha reminds us, "Throughout Disciples history, there has been considerably more diversity in the midst of the fragile unity of our church than our history books would indicate."[1]

Black, Latine, and Asian Disciples contributed to a church that was often ambivalent about their place in the church and in society. We should aim to tell the many diverse histories of Disciples—note the plural—and resist the urge to tell a single narrative. The unity of Disciples history lives in tension with our diversity. What follows then is not "the story of

[1] Sandhya Jha, *Room at the Table: Struggle for Unity and Equality in Disciples History* (St. Louis, MO: Chalice Press, 2009), 1.

Disciples" but an attempt to highlight some of the "turning points" in our history.

Disciples are often referred to as "people of the parenthesis," mostly because of our name. However, it is probably more accurate to say we are a "people of the paradox," willing to hold together seemingly oppositional ideas. As Michael Kinnamon reminds us, "At our best, we are both-and people in an either-or world, a community that insists on holding in tension what others split apart."[2] This was true from the very origins of the movement.

Disciples did not emerge from a single source but from two very different contexts: revivalism and immigration. Two foundational documents in the first decade of the nineteenth century bear witness to these diverse origins. In 1804, Barton W. Stone and five colleagues penned and signed a document titled *The Last Will and Testament of the Springfield Presbytery*. Shaped by their experience of the 1801 revival at Cane Ridge (Kentucky), *The Last Will and Testament* is a foundational document in American history for religious liberty. A few years later, in 1809, Thomas Campbell, a recent emigrant from Ireland soon joined by his son, Alexander, published the *Declaration and Address* in Washington County, Pennsylvania. Influenced by Thomas's experience with the Evangelical Society of Ulster (Ireland), this document promoted two

[2] Michael Kinnamon, "The People of the Paradox" (lecture, National City Christian Church (Disciples of Christ), Washington, D.C., April 24, 2009), 1, Michael Kinnamon Papers (PP-00144), Box 1, Folder 7, Disciples of Christ Historical Society, Bethany, WV.

ideals: the restoration of New Testament Christianity and the achievement of Christian unity. Together, these documents testify to the American and transatlantic origins of the movement. They also embody one of the persistent paradoxes in our history—the tension between unity and liberty.

Although the leaders of the two movements, Alexander Campbell and Barton Stone, disagreed on numerous points over the next two decades, they eventually supported the union of the two groups, the Christians (Stoneites) and the Disciples (Campbellites), which occurred on January 1, 1832, in Lexington, Kentucky. The Stone-Campbell movement experienced tremendous growth in the following decades, expanding from about 22,000 members in 1832 to nearly 200,000 by the start of the Civil War. During this time, Alexander Campbell became the movement's leading voice, shaping its theology, organizational structure, and public discourse, primarily through his periodical, *The Millennial Harbinger*. Just a couple of years after the union, the first African American congregation, the Colored Christian Church, was established in 1854. Black Disciples were forging their own identity. In some racially mixed churches, Black members served as exhorters, even while many White Disciples remained uncertain about their inclusion.

Although not clearly evident then, the Civil War profoundly reshaped the movement. As historian Mark Noll has observed, the Civil War constituted nothing less than a "theological crisis" for American Protestants in the nineteenth century, and this was certainly true for our movement, which included both abolitionists and proslavery Christians.[3] Disciples did not formally split over the "slavery question" as other denominations did in the 1850s/1860s, but the war's sectional divisions would result in the first major split in the movement.

By the dawn of the twentieth century, the break was apparent. The 1906 Federal Religious Census listed two distinct groups from the Stone-Campbell movement: Disciples of Christ, concentrated in the upper Midwest, and Churches of Christ, based primarily in the former Confederate states. A movement born of a vision for Christian unity had experienced major division.

In the half-century between the Civil War and World War I, the second generation of Disciples pursued cooperation in foreign and domestic mission work by forming numerous societies. The move toward cooperation originated before the Civil War with the establishment of the American Christian Missionary Society (ACMS) in 1849. This was followed by the formation of the Christian Woman's Board of Missions (CWBM), the Foreign Christian Missionary Society (FCMS), and the National Benevolent Association (NBA) in the 1870s. Women played a leading role in founding these societies and made real efforts to honor the church's diversity. The CWBM opened a Chinese mission in Portland, Oregon, in 1891; and the ACMS welcomed the first Spanish-language Christian Church in San Antonio in 1899. The "society era" built connections with the broader society and cooperation

---

[3] Mark Noll, *The Civil War as a Theological Crisis* (University of North Carolina Press, 2006), 6.

with other Christian bodies. When the Federal Council of Churches was established in the first decade of the twentieth century, Disciples were charter members.

The next major turning point occurred between the years 1917 and 1919. In the ongoing search for a more efficient organizational structure, two conventions were established in 1917: first, the predominantly White International Convention and, second, the National Christian Missionary Convention (NCMC), created by African American Disciples to institutionalize a Black Disciples identity among its churches. Two years later, in 1919, the United Christian Missionary Society (UCMS) was created, consolidating the work of several societies into a single mission-oriented organization. This era was marked both by increased organization—what Disciples historian D. Duane Cummins has described as Disciples' "drive to maturity"—and growing dissatisfaction among churches seeking more independence.[4] This divide would lead to the second major division in the movement, a break completed in the 1960s.

In the years following World War II, Disciples sought to cooperate more with other Christian bodies but encountered roadblocks because of organizational confusion. In response, in the 1950s, a panel of scholars was commissioned to study the identity and thought of Disciples. The panel report led to a "Commission on Brotherhood Restructure" in 1960, once again seeking a new organizational structure for a new era.

[4] D. Duane Cummins, *A Handbook for Today's Disciples,* 3rd ed. (St. Louis: Chalice Press, 2017), 11.

Through the process of "Restructure," Disciples eventually approved the "Provisional Design for the Christian Church (Disciples of Christ)" in 1968, marking its transformation into a full-fledged denomination. The following year, the International Convention (White Disciples) and the National Christian Missionary Convention (Black Disciples) adopted the "Merger Agreement," completing more than two decades of efforts to come together.

In the decades since Restructure and the Merger Agreement, Disciples have sought to recognize the diversity of the church in its organizational structure. This included the organization of the Fellowship of Asian American Disciples in 1976, which became the North American Pacific/Asian Disciples (NAPAD) in 1996, and the establishment of the National Hispanic and Bilingual Fellowship in 1981 and Central Pastoral Office for Hispanic Ministries in 1992, now known as *Obra Hispana*.

A lot can be said about Disciples history, but we do not have room for that here. What I will say about the turning points outlined above is this: At each juncture, Disciples have wrestled with who we are, learning and relearning that faithfulness means not escaping our tensions and differences but inhabiting them. It is in embracing diversity—not despite our vision for Christian unity, but as its expression—that we glimpse the church God is calling us to become.

Global Ministries

LaMarco Cable

In 2024, the Division of Overseas Ministries (DOM), doing business as Disciples Overseas Ministries, celebrated 175 years of transformative missional history. This milestone invites the Christian Church (Disciples of Christ) to reflect on the evolution of its global mission—one that has shifted from a traditional evangelistic model to a dynamic, mutual partnership, culminating in the formation of Global Ministries, a shared witness with the United Church of Christ (UCC).

Disciples first sent missionaries to Jerusalem in 1849, followed by India in 1874, China in 1890, and the Congo (now the Democratic Republic of the Congo) in 1899. These early efforts focused on spreading Christianity through church planting, education, and healthcare, reflecting a nineteenth-century understanding of mission as bringing the gospel to distant lands. Although these efforts laid the foundation for a global Disciples presence, they also embodied a one-directional approach, in which mission was understood as

Western Christians bringing faith and God to others, rather than engaging in a mutual relationship.

By the mid-twentieth century, a growing awareness emerged that mission should not be about imposing beliefs but, rather, about engaging in reciprocal relationships with churches and communities worldwide. Former "mission fields" became strong, independent churches with their own theological insights and leadership. This shift led to a redefinition of mission—from one of conversion to one of solidarity, justice, and accompaniment.

Reflecting this shift, Disciples and the UCC no longer use the term "missionary," which has historically implied a one-way transfer of faith and resources. Instead, we refer to those serving in international ministry as "mission co-workers," emphasizing their role as partners who listen, learn, and serve alongside global communities rather than over them.

In 1996, DOM took a significant step forward by joining with the UCC's Wider Church Ministries to form Global Ministries—a common witness to God's mission in the world. This ecumenical partnership affirmed that mission is not about bringing God to others but about discovering God already at work in every culture and context.

Global Ministries prioritizes justice, mutuality, and reconciliation, engaging in mission by walking alongside international partners in areas such as peace building, sustainable development, disaster relief, and leadership training. Today, we collaborate with two hundred and fifty global partners in ninety countries, working together for a world in which all people experience God's love and justice.

Although Global Ministries is a partnership of Disciples and the UCC, our global partners are not limited to these denominations. Many of our partners are from different Christian traditions and faith backgrounds, brought together by a shared commitment to missional alignment rather than by denominational identity. This reflects a deep conviction that God's mission transcends institutional boundaries and calls us to work together for justice, peace, and human dignity.

Recognizing that true partnership requires shared decision making, Global Ministries has prioritized the leadership of international partners. Six international partners serve as board members, ensuring that mission is shaped and guided by those engaged in ministry on the ground. This commitment reflects a deep desire to decenter Western dominance in mission and move toward a model of co-creation and mutual leadership.

In November 2024, Global Ministries affirmed four organizational priorities that will guide its future work:

1. Leadership development: Investing in theological education, capacity building, and the next generation of faith leaders worldwide.
2. Decolonization: Dismantling colonial structures in mission, promoting equitable partnerships, and affirming the wisdom and agency of global partners.

3. Transformative and authentic global engagement: Strengthening mission relationships rooted in mutuality, justice, and deep listening.
4. Empowerment for action: Equipping congregations and individuals for active participation in global justice work.

As DOM marks its 175th anniversary in 2024, Disciples celebrate the legacy of those who have shaped this ministry and embrace the vision of mission as a partnership of equals. From its early evangelistic beginnings to its present-day commitment to global justice and collaboration, DOM's journey reflects an evolving and deepening understanding of what it means to be Christ's witnesses in the world.

Congregations and Their Pastors

Katie Hays

A congregation is a group of Christians who embody their discipleship of Jesus together. Congregations can be small or large; financially broke or well-funded; homogenous in race, ethnicity, and language group, or diverse in all those ways. They can be traditional in worship practice or experimental with music, prayer, and preaching. Their members can occupy the conserving or liberating ends of the social-political spectrum in an energizing mix of perspectives, or they can be more culturally congruent with one another.

Congregations within the Christian Church (Disciples of Christ) vary widely in all these ways and more. As the saying goes, if you know one DOC congregation, you know one DOC congregation.

There are some commonalities you can expect from local DOC congregations, however. This is not an exhaustive list, but broadly this is what congregations do:

1. Worship: Congregations provide an enriching rhythm of worship. They organize opportunities

for people to connect their hearts to the heart of God, and invite the participation of all in worship, baptism, and the Lord's supper. Although it is possible to join your praise with the song of all creation (Psalm 65) when you're all alone, most of us need a plan (a.k.a., liturgy) and some companions for the work of worship.

2. Prayer: Congregations help their people pray. Again, you don't *need* anyone's intervention to speak with God. But most of us find that we often don't know what to say, or we get bogged down in our own worries and frustrations, so that prayer becomes a chore. Congregations offer chances for their people to join together in prayer so that no one is left out of our ongoing conversation with God.
3. Theological thinking: Congregations think about God together. With diligence and humility, Jesus' followers read the Bible, listening to the voices of our ancestors in faith. New thoughts about God, God's world, and ourselves in God's world are always available; by definition, human beings will never settle all the questions. The Spirit provokes new imaginings, prodding us to let go of outdated or harmful theology. Collective discernment helps individuals engage courageously with what God is doing now, and what God is doing next.

4. Friendship: Congregations solve the problem of loneliness. In a culture that is increasingly fragmented, the local church provides a safe space for vulnerable people to connect for companionship. There is no need to hide or pretend; the local church at its best is ready to receive each person who crosses its threshold with the very welcome of God.
5. Harmony: Congregations teach people how to love one another. When members combine and distribute their resources, discern their collective future steps, and share their lives together, there are inevitably clashes of interests. But working through differences and celebrating valuable harmony (not uniformity) is crucial to our development as Jesus' followers. By loving each other, members learn to love people beyond the circle of the congregation, so that the local church's main export is love, just the way Jesus said it should be (John 15:12–17).
6. Blessing: Congregations bless the world that God still loves. Individual believers can be committed to justice, practice mercy in their relationships, and give generously of their resources for the world's flourishing. But combining individual efforts multiplies their effect and amplifies Christ's witness in the world. Congregations join with

neighbors to strengthen local communities and to participate in God's global presence, becoming useful partners in God's ongoing work in and among the human family.

To fulfill all of these tasks, congregations build infrastructure to support their work, a kind of trellis on which a vine can grow (John 15:5). Examples of congregational infrastructure could include:

- A place to meet, sometimes called "the church" but actually just a shelter for the local church's life together.
- A bank account and a budget, or a financial framework for the careful stewardship of the congregation's combined resources.
- A leadership structure made up of paid workers and volunteers for discerning how best the congregation can partner with God in all the ways described above.
- A calendar of gatherings through which the congregation's life together happens.

It is easy for a congregation to focus overly much on the infrastructure (the trellis), as if that—the property, the money, the leadership, the programming—is the main point of the church's life. But at its best, the trellis simply (and sometimes invisibly) supports a living, growing vine that produces the good fruit of worship, prayer, theological thinking, friendship, harmony, and blessing.

Most congregations have a pastor—a person (or perhaps multiple people) ordained or commissioned for Christian ministry. In a DOC congregation, the paid ministerial staff has theological education along with the wider church's endorsement of their gifts and calling. The pastor is not the congregation's boss but its servant, a facilitator of the church's life in the ways listed above. A pastor's multiple roles include:

- Theologian-in-residence: A pastor reads the Bible, pays attention to context, and prays for discernment for the work of leading the congregation's members in their own theological formation.
- People connector: A pastor cannot be every member's confidante and caregiver. Connecting members with one another is an unselfish gift of potential relationship, so that there are no strangers in congregational life.
- Administrator: Tending to the infrastructure that makes church life possible often takes quite a lot of a pastor's time and energy. It is a form of care for the whole congregation and can be shared by church members.
- Visioner: A pastor prayerfully asks to catch a glimpse of God's vision for his or her congregation and community, and then communicates that vision, inviting members to join the fulfilling work of partnering with God.

Perhaps the most important thing to know about congregational life is that any congregation you join will be changed by your presence in it. The congregation's welcome is *not* "Come on in and do things our way" but, rather, "Who knows what God will do now that you're here?" Your partnership and participation are key to the congregation's worship, prayer, theological thinking, friendship, harmony, and blessing. We are so glad you've come.

A Brief Overview of Disciples Polity

LaTaunya Bynum

When I was a teenager, I had heard vague talk by some of the adults in my home congregation of an adjustment to what we Christian Church folks would be called. I had heard us called the Christian Church, or the Disciples of Christ, or even "The Brotherhood."

Then, one Saturday afternoon, after choir rehearsal our pastor who had recently been at an International Convention of the Christian Church, told us that we would be changing the sign on the church to read, "United Christian Church (Disciples of Christ). That was my first introduction to polity. The church had voted, the people gathered had spoken.

The definition of polity that best suits the Disciples describes polity as any group organized for governance. Polity is not an inanimate set of rules and procedures, it is how a group understands itself. Polity in the church is the people of God who have chosen to be church together.

Disciples participate in three expressions of ministry. As the online document "Our Identity/Our Structure"[1] describes us, "in the Christian Church (Disciples of Christ) congregations are connected to each other by a common covenant that continues to allow for each expression of church life (congregational, regional, and general) to be self-governing and to make decisions that are only binding upon the body that has taken the decision. Each expression thus has its own rights and responsibilities – all set within a mutual covenantal accountability."

Congregations are the foundation of the church. They are where faith communities gather for worship, community, study, and mission. Each congregation can call their own pastors, manage their budgets, programs, and properties, and participate with other Disciples and ecumenical siblings in the faith.

Regions are a collection of congregations in defined geographical areas. Regions are guided by Regional Ministers who often serve as mentors to local pastors, congregations, and clergy. They often offer training and other services to congregations as the regional governing organization sees a need.

The General church (we are the Christian Church - Disciples of Christ in the United States and Canada). The general expression of the church is dedicated to equipping

---

[1] "Our Structure," Disciples.org, accessed May 21, 2025, https://disciples.org/our-identity/our-structure/.

congregations to be and share the Good News from their doorsteps to the ends of the earth. The self-governing ministries work together to support the local congregation and regions. Congregations provide critical financial support to these ministries through Disciples Mission Fund. General Ministries are covenantally accountable to the General Board and General Assembly, providing in-depth reports, participation, and leadership to both bodies.

The General Assembly is the gathering of the church where lay, clergy, voting and nonvoting, young and old gather for worship and learning in addition to attending to the business of the Church. The voting body is made up of representatives from congregations and regions and serves as the body ministries report to in covenantal accountability. The General Assembly also operates as a forum for discussion and discernment. It can debate matters of conscience, but it cannot impose a position on a church. The assembly can request congregations, regions, and ministries to uphold policies, such as requirements for ministerial training.

Several years ago, when I was a pastor in Ohio, I was part of an inter-faith clergy group working on organizing our congregations to better serve the east side of Columbus. To get to know each other we would spend time in our meetings learning about each other's polity and practices.

On the day it was my turn to describe the Disciples, I explained that we celebrate communion every Sunday and at other times when we gather and that we baptize by immersion. I talked about our three expressions of church. I shared that lay people are empowered to lead and to do what in some other communions only clergy are allowed to do. Lay Disciples can preach, preside at the table and distribute communion, they serve as spiritual leaders and often the pastor is accountable to the congregation's board or a board of elders.

When I finished my presentation, there were questions. If lay people can do those things, who has authority? Who makes final decisions? Who decides how a congregation shares its resources with the larger body? The answer to all those questions was "we do, and we work together for the most part because we are in a covenantal relationship with each other." That is how our polity works.

Because our ministries can order much of their own lives, we sometimes hear them described as autonomous, or self-governing or independent, operating with no external accountability.

Terri Hord Owens, our General Minister and President, reminds us that we are not autonomous; rather we are self-governing and in covenant with each other.

It is not autonomy that drives us, it is covenant. In a Disciples General Board presentation a few years ago, Disciples scholar Casey Sigmon helped us understand covenant as a theological and ecclesial concept. She says: I believe in people's capacity to assemble and feast together even in disagreement and discernment. Both core affirmations felt right at home in the covenant people who call themselves Disciples of Christ.

Etymologically speaking, 'covenant' comes to us from the Latin *convenire,* meaning to convene, assemble, come together. Disciples embody covenant when they assemble- as a congregation, a region, a general church. Covenant is not just ideologically it is physiological. The body must commit to assembling.

Covenant people are lovingly bound to one another while contract people are legally bound.

Covenant is a living and loving promise or commitment between living and loving parties. It also relates to context the samc living loving care.

Covenant is a verb, theologically, not a noun. It is an agile way of following God in context, in relationship with other living things. I see this agility in the ideal of our tradition that there is no creed but Christ, thus able to think and act quickly, participating in God's work for wholeness (shalom) in a fragmented world.

Covenant people are also agile, in that when conflict comes about, when partners disagree about hard things, ideally, we work through conflict to reach a new level of understanding and a new way of being. Conflict can be the beginning of a new chapter rather than the ending of the agreement and relationship.

Our simple polity can seem complicated, but when we embody it, we are church together.

About the Editors

Rev. Dr. Kamilah Hall Sharp is assistant professor of Hebrew Bible and public ministry at Chicago Theological Seminary and a co-pastor at The Gathering, A Womanist Church in Dallas, Texas.

Dr. Joel A. Brown is president of the Disciples of Christ Historical Society in Bethany, West Virginia.

About the Contributors

Rev. Dr. Ronald J. Allen is professor of preaching, and gospels and letters, emeritus, at Christian Theological Seminary in Indianapolis, Indiana.

Rev. Dr. LaTaunya Bynum is the regional minister of the Christian Church (Disciples of Christ) of Northern California–Nevada.

Rev. Dr. LaMarco A. Cable is co-executive of Global Ministries and the president and chief executive officer of Disciples Overseas Ministries, a general ministry based in Indianapolis, Indiana.

Rev. Dr. Katie Hays is lead evangelist at Galileo Church in Fort Worth, Texas.

Rev. Dr. José Francisco Morales Torres is associate professor of comparative theology and philosophy at Chicago Theological Seminary.

Rev. Teresa Hord Owens is the general minister and president of the Christian Church (Disciples of Christ) in the United States and Canada.

Rev. Eli Rolón Jeong is associate regional minister for children, youth, and young adults in the Living Waters Region of the Christian Church (Disciples of Christ).

Rev. Nathan Russell is senior pastor of Washington Avenue Christian Church (Disciples of Christ) in Elyria, Ohio.

Rev. Paul S. Tché is president of the Christian Unity and Interfaith Ministry (CUIM), a Disciples' general ministry based in Indianapolis, Indiana.

Rev. Dr. Christopher Wilson is senior pastor of St. Andrew Christian Church (Disciples of Christ) in Olathe, Kansas.

For Further Reading

Boring, M. Eugene. *Disciples and the Bible: A History of Disciples Biblical Interpretation in North America.* St. Louis: Chalice Press, 1997.

Cardwell, Brenda M., and Fox, William K., Sr. *Journey Toward Wholeness: A History of Black Disciples of Christ in the Mission of the Christian Church.* St. Louis: Chalice Press, 1990.

Cartwright, Colbert. *People of the Chalice: Disciples of Christ in Faith and Practice.* St. Louis: Chalice Press, 1997.

Cummins, D. Duane. *The Disciples: A Struggle for Reformation.* 2nd ed. St. Louis: Chalice Press, 2023.

Cummins, D. Duane. *A Handbook for Today's Disciples.* 5th ed. St. Louis: Chalice Press, 2017.

Cummins, D. Duane, translation by Conchia Delgado. *Un Manual para los Discípulos de Hoy en la Iglesia Cristiana (Discipulos de Cristo).* St. Louis: Chalice Press, 1999.

Heltzel, Peter Goodwin, ed. *Chalice Introduction to Disciples Theology.* St. Louis: Chalice Press, 2008.

Jha, Sandhya. *Room at the Table: Struggle for Unity and Equality in Disciples History.* St. Louis: Chalice Press, 2009.

Jiménez, Pablo A. *Somos Uno: Historia, teologia y gobierno de la Iglesia Cristiana (Discipulos de Cristo)*. St. Louis: Chalice Press, 2005.

Kinnamon, Michael, and Linn, Jan. *Disciples: Who We Are and What Holds Us Together*. St. Louis: Chalice Press, 2019.

Lowery, Richard H., Burnley, Lawrence A. Q., Cummins, D. Duane, and Morgan, Peter M., eds. *Seeking God's Design: Disciples' Quest for Unity and Wholeness*. St. Louis: Chalice Press, 2019.

McAllister, Lester G., and Tucker, William E. *Journey in Faith: A History of the Christian Church (Disciples of Christ)*. St. Louis: Chalice Press, 1975.

Morgan, Peter M. *Disciples Eldership: A Quest for Identity and Ministry*. St. Louis: Chalice Press, 2003.

Osborn, Ronald E. *The Faith We Affirm: Basic Beliefs of Disciples of Christ*. St. Louis: Chalice Press, 1979.

Owens, Terri Hord. *Staying at the Table: Being the Church We Say We Are*. St. Louis: Chalice Press, 2025.

Sprinkle, Stephen V. *Disciples and Theology: Understanding the Faith of a People in Covenant*. St. Louis: Chalice Press, 1999.

Toulouse, Mark G. *Joined in Discipleship: The Shaping of Contemporary Disciples Identity*. St. Louis: Chalice Press, 1997.

Williams, D. Newell, Douglas A. Foster, and Paul M. Blowers, eds. *The Stone-Campbell Movement: A Global History*. St. Louis: Chalice Press, 2013.

Wilson, Christopher W. *Passage into Discipleship: Guide to Baptism*. St. Louis: Chalice Press, 2009.

Yu, Geunhee. *A Handbook for Korean-American Disciples in the Christian Church (Disciples of Christ)*. St. Louis: Chalice Press, 2005.